10 Powerful Tips for Training

Unstoppable Children

Patti Gibble

Gibble Publishing
Tucson, Arizona

ISBN-13: 978-0615564432
ISBN-10: 0615564437

Printed in the U.S.A.

First Edition

Acknowledgements

Thank you, God, for helping me to write this book. Thank you, Mom and Dad, for loving me and taking me to church. Thanks to my husband who totally supported me throughout this journey. Thank you, Kendra, for allowing me to include your stories in this book. Thank you, June, for teaching me to write. Thank you, Linda Dowdle, for teaching me to hear the voice of God. Thank you, Tom Ulrich and David White, for believing in me and mentoring me. Thank you to all the wonderful volunteers and staff who made kids' church happen every week. Thank you, Dr. Roger Barrier, for the opportunity to serve under your leadership. Thank you, Dr. Mike Murdock for telling me to write a book. Thank you, Pastor Zane Anderson, for the title and direction you gave me with the "Unstoppable Generation" sermon. Thank you, Lucee Loy, for the photos. Thank you to all my many editors, especially Zaria Banks.

.

To the Holy Spirit–my inspiration!
Love, Patti

Contents

1.

Love – the unstoppable force!

No one can compete with the force of love. Men, women, and children cannot resist it. All our lives we pursue it. And when we find it, love brings untold pleasure.

We are instructed by God to love. Jesus said, "'Love the Lord your God with all your heart and with all your soul and with all your mind. This is the first and greatest commandment. The second is like it. Love your neighbor as yourself'" (Matthew 22:37-40). These two commandments are the greatest, and we need to obey them. However, if we give it all away–our heart, soul, and mind, in order to obey the first commandment to love God, then how can we obey the second commandment to love others, which includes our children? Well, when we bring God into the equation, by loving Him first, then the Holy Spirit comes into our hearts, fills us up with more love, and this love overflows onto others. In this way, God loves others through us!

The first powerful tip for training unstoppable children is love. Love your children like you love yourself–and that is a whole lot of love. Pour out love onto your children. Do not hold back from loving them under any circumstance, even when you have to use "tough love" the kind of love you use when you discipline your children. Unlimited love, which comes from above, is the best way to win children for the Lord. This kind of love is unstoppable!

When I first had my daughter, I really wanted to be a good parent. I wanted to do the best job I could do for her. As a new parent, I felt an enormous amount of pressure. It became a heavy burden to me and I wanted relief. It was haunting me 24/7 and I started looking for help. I found it at a ladies Bible study group. In this group I learned to ask God questions and to listen for answers. The first question I asked God was, "How do I raise my child?" and the instruction He gave me was "Love her." He just said, "Love her." Every time I prayed, I got that same answer over and over again: "Love her."

I understood instantly that it was a deep down, passionate love that God instructed me to give her. It was the kind of love God gives us when he raises us up. You may think to yourself, *yes, of course it is common sense to love your child*, but I was afraid that if I loved my child too much, I would spoil her or somehow love her more than I loved God. God knew I was worried about this issue when I asked Him how to raise her. He also knew that I was holding something back. I was holding back some love. So, when the Holy Spirit gave me permission to love my daughter fully, I felt free to really love her, the way God wanted to love her, by His Spirit, through me.

Since starting this parenting journey, love has been my guiding force. There have been lots of mistakes on my part; yet despite all my mistakes and messes, my child still knows that I love her! I may not always agree with her. I may not always be happy with her. But I always, always love her. It is a deep down, passionate love that comes from my heart to her heart. I show it every day. I let her know in every way. Where my love is limited, the Holy Spirit comes in to love on her some more.

The Bible says that "God is love" (1 John 4:8), and love is God. These two words are interchangeable. So when I say love has been my guiding force, it is the same as saying God has been my guiding force. God/love has been my guiding force on this parenting journey. God/love is the strongest force in the universe. And, God/love is the unstoppable attraction that keeps my child coming back for more. God/love has proven this over and over again.

Whatever happens between my daughter and me, love is the force that keeps us together. Therefore, love is my recommendation as the best possible way to start parenting your children. Begin today with love. Do not hold back, but lavish love on your children. Love is never, ever, ever inappropriate. Not in life, not in death, not in anything. No matter what your children do or wherever they go, they will always be drawn back to love.

"Love never fails" (1 Corinthians 13:8). When you love, you are in the no-fail zone! So then, love your children, spend time with them, and enjoy them. Love is the force that will keep them coming back to you. Love is the force that will keep your children coming back to God. God is love and love is the unstoppable force in the universe!

2.

Honor – the unstoppable blessing!

There are ten commandments in the Bible but only one commandment has a blessing attached to it. Commandment number five has been delivered to us with a blessing! This is what the Bible says: "Honor your father and mother that it may go well with you and that you may enjoy long life on earth" (Ephesians 6:2-3). As long as you honor your parents, you will live long and be blessed!

Honor is the second powerful tip for training unstoppable children. If you want your children to be lined up for this blessing, require your children to honor you. Start the process by modeling honor in your own life. First, honor God as your Heavenly Father. Next, honor your earthly father and mother. Finally, honor your children.

Pour onto your children all the honor, respect, and dignity you want poured out onto you. Even when you need to discipline them, do it with honor, not humiliation. The best way to teach your children honor is to model honor. When you give honor you can expect to get honor in return. When your children give honor to you, they will be blessed all the days of their lives. Never-ending blessing is unstoppable blessing!

When I was young, I did not practice the principle of honor. I did not know the rewards of honor. So, when I began training my daughter, I failed to teach her honor. I failed to model honor and I did not expect honor in return. As a whole, I did not embrace honor as a rule for my family. Ignorance about the principle of honor created a big problem for me and my family. I had no idea that a lack of honor was the problem. Then, one day the Lord had me focus on the problem as He highlighted it through a Bible story. The story God used to teach me the rewards of honor and the consequences of dishonor is a story of two parents who used very different parenting styles. These parents were Eli and Hannah. Here is the story:

Eli had two sons who managed to spread dishonor throughout the land of Israel. His sons did terrible things to people. Eli knew his sons were misbehaving, but he did nothing to correct their bad behavior. He even questioned his sons about their actions, but he gave them no consequences.

Eventually, God spoke to Eli about his sons' behavior through a child named Samuel. Samuel lived in the temple with Eli, the Priest of Israel. Samuel lived in the temple with Eli because he had been given to God by his mother Hannah. Hannah had made a promise to God that if He granted her request to have a son, she would give the child back to Him to serve God in the temple all the days of his life. So Hannah did just as she promised; she gave her son, Samuel, back to God to serve Him in the temple.

One night God spoke to the child Samuel three times, but Samuel did not know it was God who was speaking. Because he was so young, Samuel had not been trained to hear God's voice. He thought that Eli was calling his name, so he went to answer Eli in the middle of the night. After the third time, Eli told Samuel that it was God who was speaking to him. That night, Eli trained Samuel to answer the Lord by saying, "Yes, Lord, your servant is listening."

So in the middle of the night God talked to Samuel and told him what was going to happen to the sons of Eli because of their bad behavior. The next morning, Eli asked Samuel what God told him. Samuel reluctantly told Eli that God had said his sons would be killed. Even after being warned by God, Eli still did nothing to correct his sons' behavior or to teach them honor. Eli's sons went on doing *evil and continued to dishonor God and His people.*

At the end of the story, Eli and his sons all ended up dead on the same day as a result of his sons' dishonorable behavior! After that, the Lord raised up Samuel who showed great honor to God and His people. Samuel grew to be a great prophet and all the people looked up to Samuel for spiritual leadership.

What really stood out to me from this Bible story was that even when Eli was warned about his sons' behavior and the dire consequences that dishonor would bring, Eli did nothing to correct the problem. In short, Eli failed to discipline his sons. Then the Lord spoke to me about my family situation and asked me if I wanted to have a child like one of Eli's sons or if I wanted to have a child like Hannah's son, Samuel. I knew right away I wanted a child like Samuel, even if it meant giving my child up to God and trusting Him to show me how to discipline her. You can read the story of Eli, Hannah, and Samuel in the Bible. It is found in the first book of Samuel.

From that one Bible story, I learned the value of honor. But before I could lecture my child about honor, I needed to model honor in my own life. God began to teach me how to honor others.

The process started with me honoring my mother. My mother loved receiving cards in the mail. So, I began to honor her by sending her cards. She responded to my cards with much love and appreciation. My dad was so happy because he always wanted me to honor my mother. Later, when we traveled back to Florida to visit my family, I received the rewards of honor. My family greeted me with so much love! My Dad took us all out to lunch; we had a wonderful time together, and my mother gave me and my daughter two big, expensive pieces of jewelry!

This reward was a total surprise to me. I never saw it coming. Honor works! It worked to set me and my whole family up for a blessing. My mother is still very happy with the way I honor her. In fact, my mother wrote me a card and said that I am, "one of the best mothers in the United States!" For my mother to honor me in this way is a great blessing. Showing honor continues to set my family up for the blessing. Honoring others can set your family up for the blessing too!

Honor is an important principle for our children to practice. If you need help setting up a plan of discipline for your children in order to correct dishonorable behavior, there are many great books to check out. Dr. Kevin Leman is a psychologist and author who has written several books on discipline.

We read, we study, and take classes on many things that are important to us. Let's invest our time in studying how to raise our children and make them a top priority. If we want our children to be lined up for the blessing, we must teach them to show honor.

Honor your father and mother is a command from God. Honor brings us favor everywhere we go, and honor works to line our children up for unstoppable blessing! It is your privilege to honor your children with the blessing today.

3.

Salvation – the unstoppable gift that keeps on giving!

When my daughter was born, I fell in love with her. I loved her so much that I wanted to give her the best gift I could give her–the ultimate gift! I thought and thought about it. I prayed and prayed about it. Then one day, I asked God, "What is the best gift I could give my daughter?" God told me the best gift I could give her was the gift that Jesus had already purchased for her–the gift of salvation.

Salvation is her ticket to heaven and her escape from hell. Salvation is the gift that keeps on giving for eternity. Salvation is the third powerful tip for training unstoppable children. Salvation is forever. Realizing that it is the ultimate gift and that I could give it to her at once, I made up my mind to deliver. I was excited to share the good news.

When my child was very young I shared the message of salvation with her. First, I told her about God. I told her God is perfect, and He has never done anything wrong. I explained, He is perfect but we cannot get close to Him because we are not perfect. Being around a perfect God we feel so badly about all the wrong things that we have done. Second, I explained that doing wrong things is called sin and sin makes us feel bad about ourselves. Sin keeps us from getting close to God. Even if we only did one wrong thing in our entire life, we still have sin in our hearts.

One thing God wants us to do is obey. God said, "...children obey your parents..." (Ephesians 6:1). To obey is to do what we are told to do. If children do not obey what their parents tell them to do, it is a sin. Not obeying even one time is wrong. I gave my daughter this example: When parents ask their kids to pick up their toys and they don't do it that is a sin. Sin makes us not perfect. Then I asked my daughter if she had ever done anything wrong. She said, "Yes." I told her that is sin and sin keeps us from being with God because He is perfect. I continued explaining that we are born in sin. Our parents sinned and sin is passed down to us when we are born. Sin is what makes our spiritual hearts dirty. So because our hearts are dirty with sin, we need to have our hearts cleaned to be with God.

Then I asked her, "How do you clean a dirty heart." She thought and thought about it. We can't clean a dirty heart with soap and water, I said. The only thing that cleans a dirty heart is blood—clean, pure, perfect blood. The problem is that nobody has clean, pure, perfect blood for washing away sin because every human in the whole world has sinned—except one human. That perfect human is Jesus. He is the only one who did not sin and His blood is perfectly clean.

Finally, I shared with her that God loves us so much He is willing to help us clean our dirty hearts. God has made a way for us to clean our hearts by sending His son Jesus to die on the cross and to shed His blood for us. Then, God brought Jesus back from death to life. Now Jesus can help us clean our spiritual hearts. He can use His perfect blood, from the cross, to clean our hearts.

When we have clean hearts, we can be with God. I asked my daughter if she wanted to let Jesus clean her heart with His perfect blood she said "Yes." I led her in a prayer to accept Jesus' blood that would clean her heart and save her from being separated from God forever. By the power of the Holy Spirit, my daughter was able to understand and receive God's gift of salvation!

Even though I did not have the perfect approach for leading my child to Christ, I believed that my child could be saved at a young age and it happened. Believe that your children can be saved at a young age and it can happen. The Bible says that, "...God does not show favoritism" (Romans 2:11). He does not treat adults better than kids. He does not limit His love, relationship, or gifts to grown ups. God treats everybody fairly. He is not limited by the age, size, or maturity of anyone. God is a spirit and He speaks to the spirit in each person. God is so amazing; He can speak to anybody, anytime, anywhere–and they can understand Him!

People say they are afraid to lead children to Christ for many reasons. They say children are too young to understand, too young to make a commitment, or too young to remember the experience. I have seen the opposite. I have watched young children accept the gift of salvation readily when it was presented to them. Young children do not hesitate to accept the gift; they are teachable and they believe everything.

Besides, God says "I tell you the truth, unless you change and become like little children, you will never enter the kingdom of heaven" (Mathew 18:3). Children are already in that humbled position so they have an advantage when it comes to entrance into the kingdom of heaven. I know of many adults who received the gift of salvation when they were very young. They can retell the story to this day, and they have been committed to Christ for life!

As my child got older, she started to question her own salvation. It made me question whether she was truly saved or not. In the Bible I found the answer for my question. I read a scripture that says you need to "...continue to work out your own salvation..." (Philippians 2:12).

When my child reached the stage of life where she began to "work out" her salvation, I understood that she was "owning" her salvation or making it her own. I needed to let her do it and not be afraid. Besides, I was right there leading her in the prayer to receive Christ. I was able to review the entire experience with her. Since I remembered everything, I could share it in detail. I was also there to lead her through another prayer, a prayer of recommitment to the Lord whenever she needed it. This was an important stage of development in my child's spiritual life.

Later, when the enemy came along and lied to her, trying to fill her head with doubt about her salvation experience, I simply directed her to ask God for herself if she was saved or not. She did ask God, and He answered her. He spoke to her often, confirmed in her heart that she was going to heaven, and reassured her that her name was written down in the Lamb's Book of Life.

Walking my daughter through the process of working out her own salvation has been a delightful experience. The process has served to further strengthen her relationship with God. Any time there is an opportunity to doubt salvation there is also an opportunity to witness the truth. Any question of faith brings an opportunity to reaffirm faith. Whenever my daughter needed to, she could check in with God and gain reassurance from Him. From the point she discovered her gift, she examined her gift, she unwrapped her gift, and she embraced her gift. She was taking ownership of the best gift of all–the gift of salvation.

If you want to give your children the gift of salvation you must pray and ask the Holy Spirit how to share the plan of salvation with each child. God will give you the unique words to speak to each child individually so they can hear with their spiritual ears, understand the plan of salvation, and receive the best gift of all - the ultimate gift! If you need more help in teaching your children about the gift of salvation, this web address may be helpful http://4kids.ag.org/library/evangelism/how-to-lead-a-child.pdf. If you want to speak to somebody about salvation, the pastor/director of children's ministry at your local church may be a great resource for you.

When your children receive the gift of salvation, they get a ticket to heaven. They also become a child of God, and He becomes their Father. As their Father, God is in position to give them many additional gifts. They are qualified to live as a child of the Great King. This Great King happens to be the king of the entire universe. As His child, they have access to all the treasures He has stored up for them. They are qualified to reap all the benefits of the royal family. The storehouses of heaven are full of heavenly gifts for them to own. Salvation never stops giving for eternity. If you are looking for the ultimate gift for your children, the best gift you could give them is the gift of salvation.

4.

The Holy Spirit – the unstoppable friend!

The Holy Spirit is the third person in the Trinity and He is the one who is equipped to have an intimate relationship with your child. He is the only person who knows your child better than you do. He loves your child more than you could even begin to. The Holy Spirit is the only one who will never, ever leave your child alone. Remember, you only have them for a short time on earth but the Holy Spirit can be with them forever. The Holy Spirit is the fourth powerful tip for training unstoppable children.

You can't go everywhere with your child. The Holy Spirit is the only person who is capable of doing that. Besides, it would be very embarrassing for you to go everywhere with them. However, the Holy Spirit can go everywhere they go without it being a problem. To have a Friend for your child who never, ever leaves them alone is a dream come true. The Holy Spirit is the kind of Friend who would give up His life for your child and He is unstoppable!

"Greater love has no one than this that he lay down his life for his friends" (John 15:13). This Friend will join in the fight, to the death, against the enemy of your child's soul. Invite your child to unite with the Holy Spirit in friendship. When you and your child connect with the Holy Spirit, you create a powerful union. The Bible says, "A cord of three strands is not quickly broken" (Ecclesiastes 4: 12). You, your child, and the Holy Spirit create a bond that cannot be easily broken. The three amigos!

In this unity your child's power for fighting the enemy is immediately amped up and winning the battle is inevitable. An unstoppable friendship like this is the key to living a supernatural life.

Introduce each of your children to the Holy Spirit and you will never have to worry about them again. Introduce them to their best Friend. If you want the Holy Spirit involved in your child's life, pray this prayer:

Holy Spirit, thank you for (name each child as you pray for them). I give him/her back to you. I dedicate him/her to you. I ask you to be a friend to my child. I ask you to stay with my child to help them. I ask you to help me to help them. Please show me how to raise him/her to be whatever you want him/her to be right now and in their future, in Jesus' name. Amen.

Now, ask the Holy Spirit to speak to you about how to train each one of your children.

Take some time right now to listen to the Holy Spirit.

When you listen to the Holy Spirit, expect Him to speak to you. Write down whatever He tells you. You must identify who is speaking to you when you listen. If the Holy Spirit is talking to you, He will speak to you in love and with a still, small voice. If the enemy is speaking he will always speak in fear! Everything the enemy says is based in fear and confusion. In addition, you will find that you sometimes talk to yourself in your own head. You can recognize when you talk to yourself because you sound something like this: *I think I'll do this or that.*

If you listen and pay attention to the Holy Spirit, you will find that He speaks in many ways. He speaks through His written Word (the Bible). He speaks through ideas, dreams, visions, and people. Those are just a few of the ways He speaks. He never tells you to do things that go against the principles of the Bible. Do what the Holy Spirit tells you to do because He is your best friend; you can trust Him; and your children can trust Him.

The Holy Spirit is much more than just a friend to your children. He is a teacher, counselor, and helper all wrapped up in one person. Those are just some of the roles He plays in your children's lives. The Holy Spirit is the only one who knows how to train up each child. Every child is unique and the Holy Spirit is the only one who understands them completely.

Before I trained my daughter to listen to the voice of the Holy Spirit, I learned how to listen myself. Then, I taught her how to listen. After that I taught my daughter's friends how to hear the voice of God. Finally, I taught other children how to hear God's voice.

Working with children and teaching them to hear the voice of God has been an awesome experience. The children I taught heard amazing things directly from the Holy Spirit. For many, experiencing God speaking to them was awesome. For some, listening to God became a lifestyle. For others, following the Holy Spirit was so revolutionary that it brought change to their entire family. When children obtain a relationship with the Holy One, it will change their world!

Parents, you can do amazing things when the Holy Spirit is involved. You and the Holy Spirit can co-parent your children together. When you partner with the Holy Spirit, you can discover how to train your children for everyday life, for their future career, and for their ministry to others. When you join forces with the God of the universe, together you, your children, and the Holy Spirit will be the unstoppable team you've always wanted to be.

Learn more about the Holy Spirit so you can teach your children and encourage them in their relationship with Him. Teach them to love and honor Him. Teach your children to listen and obey Him. Show your children by modeling your relationship with Him every day. As you turn to the Holy Spirit for answers, you can lead your children to do the same thing.

Train your children to engage the Holy Spirit and then pray that He reveals Himself to them. Cultivate a relationship with the two of them like you do with any other person that you want involved in your children's lives. Arrange time for play dates together with the Holy Spirit. Praise, worship, and thanksgiving are great ways to invite the Holy Spirit to come out and play with you and your kids. He is the best friend–the one you have always dreamed of for you children and He is unstoppable!

5.

Relationship – the unstoppable unity that multiplies power!

An old African proverb states, "It takes a village to raise a child." That is true! A village is a small community of people, and a church is a small community of people. People come together in a community for a reason. When people work together, they get more done. You might say to yourself, *Well, I am the only person my child is going to need.* That's not true! You need to multiply your numbers through relationship in order to get a job done—the job of raising your child.

In the Bible God says, "...Christ is the head of the church, His body" (Ephesians 5:23). "Christ is the head." That means He is in charge. The Bible also says "...so in Christ we who are many form one body..." (Romans 12:5). The church is the body. That means that we (the church) work together just like the members of a body work together. A body functions better when all the members work together. That is why we need many people to work together and help us to "raise a child." Relationship is the fifth powerful tip for training unstoppable children.

First, we need children the same age as ours to play with them. Children learn by playing. I remember when I brought other kids into my house. I did it because my daughter is an only child and I wanted her to gain good social skills. But she received many more benefits than I had anticipated.

It is true, many parents already have multiple children in their own households, but not every parent sees the importance of the relationship in creating unity. They may not know the rewards of working together as the body to gain multiplied power.

When other kids came into my home, I took the opportunity to unite these children and have them learn how to be the body of Christ. I taught them how to worship God together. I taught the kids how to hear the voice of God together. I also taught them how to "play" church together in my home. These kids were completely united when they did all of these things. They always functioned in peace and harmony. When they worked together as the body of Christ, there was no fighting, screaming, or jealousy.

They played church so well that they were actually experiencing it and I was not fully aware of it at the time. This relationship was such a powerful experience that when they worked together in unity, under the anointing of the Holy Spirit, things happened. Prayers were answered and God was in the mix.

For example, my daughter and her friend "J" played baptism in the kiddy pool at the swimming area. I taught them how baptism was done in church and they played it often. Then, when my daughter got older and wanted to get baptized in "big church" her friend "J" found out and his reaction was, "What for, I already baptized her (in the swimming pool)?" Now that's what I call church! And, it happened when the children were playing together.

Other times the children had communion together. We used grape juice and tortillas and read scripture about communion. I taught them to do communion like they do in "big church." It was so powerful when the children had communion. They really confessed their sins, talked about the sacrifice Jesus, and took a moment to think about what He had done for them. Communion became so important to them that they asked to do it on a regular basis!

The children listened to God together and were getting some answers. One time when I was seeking an answer to the question: should I go back to work or not? I wanted to get the kids involved in prayer because they got answers fast. I had already asked God and He told me He would give me an answer at the end of the day. Well, I wanted an answer now and so I immediately gathered up all the children in my house, took them to my prayer room, and asked them to help me hear God's voice.

I did not tell them for what I was asking; I just said I wanted an answer from God right now. They listened and when they were done, one of the children told me that God was not ready to tell me yet. I was shocked and happy at the same time. That answer from a child confirmed two things: God would tell me the answer at the end of the day, and those kids did indeed hear the voice of God!

Next, we need to connect our children to younger children. Our children can teach them in the ways of the Lord. When older kids teach younger kids, it helps the older children to master the subject they are teaching. Also, when our children are teaching younger ones, they can see God working in the lives of those children. Those experiences tend to secure their faith.

From the time my daughter was three years old, she led children in church. First, she helped lead toddlers in preschool. Then, she advanced to lead kids in worship. Finally, she helped lead teams in church. She started her leadership training by participating in puppet plays, acting out Bible skits, telling Bible stories, running church games, and setting up kids' church programs. She became skilled in many areas and accomplished all this before she was a teenager. She was setting an example of how kids can serve in church and was learning at the same time. Her role in leadership helped her to grow and empowered her to become a leader in church, school, and many other areas of life. I trace her success back to the time she spent leading the little children in preschool.

Lastly, we need to connect our children to older children, teens, and/or young adults. This will help our children to get to the next level in their spiritual growth. We need to make sure the older ones are great role models, they are following God, and most importantly that they are safe for our children. Older children, teens, and young adults can help to multiply the amount of training our kids receive in spiritual matters. These mentors become especially important to our children when they are entering their preteen to teen years. These role models bring their own unique experiences with them and, in turn, teach our children something new each time they work with them.

They can love our children and minister to them in ways we are not be able to do. We need these people in our children's lives to challenge them to grow.

Our children will also need mature Christians to look up to, to trust, and to respect as mentors. Once again, we must make sure these adults are safe for our kids. Of course, we parents need to be good role models for our children. Grandparents, aunts and uncles may also be excellent adult mentors. All these mature Christians help to teach them how to be mighty men and women of God. To empower our children for life, we must unite with them in the body of Christ.

In order to seal our children's future, join in prayer with other adults. My daughter had adults who prayed for her when she was a child, and these adults continue to pray for her today. When we unite with other believers in prayer, these prayers will be answered because the Bible says, "...if two of you agree on earth about anything you ask for, it will be done..." (Matthew 18:19). Unity multiplies our prayer power!

We need other believers to help us, "Train a child in the way he should go..." (Proverbs 22:6). The body of Christ plays an important role in the training of our children. We need younger, older, and same-age children in their lives. We also need teens and adults to join with us in training our children. Remember never leave kids alone with anybody who is not safe. At the end of the day, prayer partners are essential for enabling us to multiply power for our children. Relationship is a powerful tip for creating unstoppable unity that multiplies power!

6.

The Church – the unstoppable fortress!

We need to protect our children! Children are not adults. They are not small grown-ups. Children are immature and we need to shelter them. The Church helps us to protect our children from being overpowered by the gates of hell. The Bible says "...I will build my church, and the gates of Hades will not overcome it" (Matthew 16:18). The Church is the body of believers Satan cannot defeat with his hellish ways. Get your children in the place where they are safe from the gates of hell. Get them to church!

The church is the sixth powerful tip for training unstoppable children. Make church a priority. Go every week if you can and keep going as much as possible. This kind of commitment to church attendance will bring protection over your children. The Church is the family of believers God has for us. Church is important to God. So if church is important to God, church must be important to us. The Church is a strong fortress set up by God that will stop the enemy in his tracks!

When my daughter was young I wanted so much for her to be protected from all harm. I thought that if she had enough money it would protect her. I thought that getting a good education would line her up for a better job, and a better job would line her up for wealth, and wealth would bring her protection. I was wrong!

One day the Lord showed me my mistake. He said to me, "Patti, you have your priorities mixed up. Education should not be your top priority. I (God) should be your top priority!" So, I believed what God said, and I changed. I made God the number-one priority for my daughter. I shifted my thinking from education being the top priority to God being the top priority for my daughter.

Because God corrected me early on, I made going to church more important than going other places. As a family, we went to church more than we went anywhere else except home. Our family attended church, volunteered at church, and socialized at church. After a while I volunteered so much at church that they offered me a job and I was eventually hired to be at church several hours a day. Then my daughter started attending the school in that church. We spent much of our time at church and we loved it.

I knew that some other families were struggling to make it to church. Church was important to them but it was not at the top of the list. I saw families struggle with sports being the top priority, school being the top priority, and even extended family being the top priority. It was amazing that because church was a lower priority to them, they ended up hardly ever attending. It was like the enemy used the other priorities any time he could to distract and prevent these families from making it to church. Eventually, when the kids grew up and went off to college, they chose not to attend church. The parents were completely shocked and surprised at the choice their kids made.

Why were these parents surprised? The children saw their parents choose sporting events, family gatherings, or various other activities over church on a regular basis. They got out of their children what they put into them. They had raised kids with mixed-up priorities.

We need to remember that kids are immature, vulnerable, and in need of spiritual direction. Kids do not always make good choices in life. We are in position, as parents, to protect our children. We are called to be the spiritual covering for our children. We must think past the soccer season, the numerous activities, and the extended family obligations.

We must help children make the right choices especially when it comes to God taking His rightful place in our lives–first place. When we put God first, He will put us first. He will change our lives for the better. Then we qualify to reap the benefits of a life with proper priorities.

I really don't want to condemn anybody. I know we all have occasions where we honestly can not make it to church. We can not go on some Sundays. We get sick, or we are on vacation and have to miss church. That being said, regular church attendance is important because it shows our kids what to value in life. Therefore, I strongly urge you to pray about every important choice you make for your children. Help them to maintain proper priorities through modeling the right order in your own life. Ask God for help.

The Holy Spirit will answer your prayers. He will guide you in making these decisions as you strive to put your life in order. The Holy Spirit will help you to put God first. Attending church is a good choice. Church provides a fortress for you and your children.

After you have prayed and decided to bring your children to church on a regular basis, you will want to keep them in church. You need to select a church carefully. Find a church that your whole family can enjoy. Find a church where your family can get connected with other believers, various programs, and service opportunities. Ultimately church should become an essential part of life for your family.

You need to ask the Holy Spirit to direct you to a church that is just right for each member of your family. Look for a church that has programs for both adults and kids. Do not just choose a church that is great for the adults in your family. The "big church," may have a great preacher, but you need to look beyond that one service to other ministries.

Please do not consider dragging your kids into "big church" if they are not engaged in the worship, and the service is not "family friendly." What a mistake! We would never think of dragging an adult man into a preschool classroom, sticking a toy in his hand, and expecting him to get something out of the lesson unless he was teaching it. So then why do we drag our preschoolers into the adult service every Sunday, ask them to be perfectly quiet for an hour, and expect them to get something out of that church service?

Even though your children may be very quiet during the service, it does not mean they have learned anything. These services are not geared for children unless there are special adjustments made on the part of the pastor. I am not saying that I don't believe in miracles. God could do a miracle, and the children could understand everything in the service because The Holy Spirit can do anything. But have you ever considered that God has already done a miracle by providing a classroom for your children where the program is tailored to meet their needs and He is allowing you to take advantage of it?

If you want to be together with your children, it is much easier for you to go into their age-appropriate classroom as a teacher or assistant. As a leader you can teach, they can learn, and you can both profit from your time spent together. When you take your children to church programs that are tailored to their specific age and attention span, you are increasing the chances of their having a good experience in church.

It is not my intention to make anyone feel guilty for what they have or have not done in the past. Everyone has to change up their routine from time to time so do not feel badly if you have been taking your kids to "big church." It is better than not taking them to church at all. Maybe it's time to change your routine a little and look into a great kids' church program for your children.

When you are looking for an appropriate church, get the whole family involved.

Consider different churches and look at all the programs within each church. When it comes to the kids' programs, think safety first! Make sure there is a procedure for the staff to check up on new teachers and workers who volunteer in the programs. These procedures ensure you that the workers can be trusted with your children. Not everybody in the church is safe and you need to be very careful to protect your children. Also make sure there is a "check in" and "check out" procedure for all the kids' programs, so no one can pick up your children except you. Next, get permission to visit all the programs for kids. You need to make sure the kids' programs are high quality. How else are you going to know this information unless you go and observe it for yourself?

I am not saying the programs for kids have to be flawless, because it is volunteers (not paid staff) who usually run all the programs at a church. What I am saying is that you don't want to put your kids in programs that are poorly staffed, low quality, or not Bible-based. Ask yourself some important questions. Are the programs age-appropriate, kid-friendly, and do they offer a variety of methods for engaging children in learning? Most of all you need to know if the programs are Spirit led. If the Holy Spirit is not a major influence in that church, you don't want your kids to be influence by that church.

Once you have decided the kids' programs meet the needs of your children, look for a Spirit-directed pastor and dynamic worship for the adults in your family. It is much easier to adjust your standards than for your children to have to endure a poor quality children's program. Once you have found a great worship service, look further to see if there are opportunities given to plug into the church.

Try to find a church that offers some connecting programs like Bible studies, kids' clubs, and/or family socials. You may need to dig deep to find out what they have to offer that will meet the needs of your family but it is well worth your time. Besides, if you take time to find out about schools, sports, and neighborhoods before moving into a new home, why not take time to find out about a church you might consider joining.

Finally, choose a church that engages their youth in programs especially if you want your kids to grow up at that church and continue attending. That is very important. Choosing a church with a great youth program is essential in the teen years, but I won't get into that subject because I would need to write a whole new book on it. There are many great books already available on the subject of raising teens. You need to obtain some of these books sooner rather than later.

Finding a good church may be a challenge for you. You may be thinking, "*Well, I live in a small town and I can not find the right church that fits all the needs of my family.*" You are fortunate because you are a part of the body of Christ that makes up the church. For all you know you may be the missing body part that makes the difference in your church. If the church has some good things to offer but not everything you need, see what you can do to help fix the problem. For example, if the church has a great main service for adults but no kids' church program, offer to start a program yourself.

Many pastors would love to have somebody help them start a great kids' church. And with this book as your resource, I know you can start a great one. Just use the same powerful tips in this book for the kids in your church. If the church has everything but social events, offer to host some socials yourself. Events are not very hard to execute, especially if you meet at a nearby park. You can have pot luck meals, social time, games, and sports for the entire family at the park.

If there is no mission outreach at your church, I bet you can think of a few needy people in town that you might be able to help right now. By doing this, you enable the church to launch a new mission ministry.

There are many things you can do to help make your church exactly what you need it to be. When you help your local church, you help yourself, your family, and the body of Christ.

By being a problem solver, you are functioning as an important member of the body of Christ that makes up the local church. You are helping your church to become a mighty fortress–one that cannot be stopped–a fortress that offers your kids safety in a very dangerous world!

7.

Discernment – the unstoppable revealer of the enemy and his lies!

Children know they have an enemy because the enemy attacks them when they are really young. The enemy does not play fair when it comes to our children. He does not say to himself, *"Ah, these children are way too little to defend themselves so I'll leave them alone for now."* No way! He waits until we are not looking and then he steps in to capture their hearts, minds, and souls.

The Bible says Satan is the father of lies. He is a liar–that's his identity. Satan's weapon is his tongue and he fights with his words. He speaks and uses his words to spread lies every day, and he hopes our kids will believe his lies. He lies to them often. He harasses them in their minds and tries to scare them. However, we don't need to be afraid of the devil because he has been defeated by Jesus on the Cross. When we are covered in the blood of Jesus, we have great authority and power! When we use discernment we are able to identify the enemy and stop his lies. Discernment is the seventh powerful tip for training unstoppable children.

Children are greatly influenced by what they hear repeatedly and they come to believe these ideas to be true. When the father of lies shows up, we need to expose him as our enemy so we have a chance to defeat him. We should not scare our children by revealing the devil to them before they are ready. No, just wait for the right time, and sure enough he will show up in your house as an uninvited guest. He identifies him self in evil words, bad dreams, and ugly attitudes.

If the enemy is speaking lies to your children, then fight back! You fight him with the truth. The Bible says "...know the truth and the truth will set you free" (John 8:32)! You can learn the truth by reading the Bible. So when the enemy tells a lie, you can counter him with the truth. You need to face the demons in your own life first. Conquer those demons and then lead your children to conquer the demons they are facing. You can teach your kids how to fight the enemy with the truth.

I caution you to be very careful when you are talking to your children about this subject and do not scare them! You will know when your children are in battle with the enemy. Some kids are attacked by nightmares when they sleep. Some kids are bothered by mean thoughts during the day time. They may behave in very unusual ways. Sometimes bazaar statements may come out of their mouths. They may not even understand what they are saying or doing at the time but it is important to pay attention. Here is an example of the enemy speaking to a child:

When my daughter was about 3 years old, we were leaving our perfect little house to start our perfect little day when something not-so-perfect happened. On our way out the door, my daughter saw the Christmas lights on our house and commented on how daddy had put up the lights. What she said after that shocked and alarmed me. She made this statement: "Daddy's dead."

Of course, I immediately responded by telling her daddy was fine. He was not dead but we needed to pray for him. Then I reassured her that God would take care of Daddy. After my daughter said those shocking words, "Daddy's dead," I heard the enemy speaking to me saying, "It's true; he's dead."

I knew he was lying to me. I also realized that my daughter did not normally talk about death. She was too young to even understand the concept of death, and we did not talk about death because we did not want to scare her. Her thoughts about daddy could not have originated in her mind. I also knew that God would not put such dreadful thoughts into my daughter's head. As I looked at my daughter in her little car seat, I suddenly got a picture of the enemy whispering lies into her ear. I was so mad! The enemy had exposed himself for one split second and I recognized him. That was a big mistake on his part. When he whispered into my daughter's ear, I recognized the enemy! That mistake set him up for a downfall in her life.

I thought to myself, *"Devil, if you are going to come after my daughter, I am going to arm her with weapons to fight you so hard it will make your head spin."* And I did. First, I taught my daughter to discern who was speaking to her. I taught her that not only could she hear my voice and God's voice, but she could also hear the enemy's voice. I was very careful not to scare her. The enemy had already shocked her and I needed to calm her down. She had learned a little about the devil from Bible stories. She knew I was talking about him when I referred to the enemy and I helped her to make the connection between him and his voice. I identified the enemy as the one who spoke into her ear and lied to her saying that daddy was dead.

I did not scare her, but assured her that it was so easy to make the enemy leave. She only needed to say the name of Jesus to make him run away in fear. I also told her that the name of Jesus would scare any of her enemies away including people that might attempt to do mean things to her. I assured her that she could say the name of Jesus over and over again until she felt secure. And if she could not say His name, she could think about Jesus and He would make her mind feel better. That day I managed to arm my daughter with the weapon of truth. She had a weapon in her mouth that could cut off the enemy's lies. We both felt better after that little lesson, or should I say that big lesson!

Later, the enemy tried to harass my child when she was asleep. My daughter began having nightmares. At that point I was able to spend more time talking to her about what she was doing right before she went to bed. I asked her what she thought about, looked at, or watched on TV before she went to bed. We got rid of any of the things that might make her feel scared and replaced them with things that made her feel safe.

We prayed together before she fell asleep, and asked God to turn the nightmares into good dreams. We also began a new bedtime routine where I told her all kinds of wonderful Bible stories. I made sure that the Bible stories were "kid-friendly stories" that made her feel safe at night: Stories like the birth of Jesus, or the promotion of Esther to be queen, or Solomon's building the temple. If she had nightmares in the middle of the night, we prayed and asked God to replace the bad pictures with good pictures from the Holy Spirit. Then she focused on the good pictures as she fell back asleep. Over the weeks I watched as her bad nightmares turned into good dreams.

To top it all off, I helped her interpret the God-given dreams. That took her to a whole new level. In the mess of it all, I remembered this Bible verse, "And we know that in all things God works for the good of those who love him, who have been called according to his purpose" (Romans 8:28). In all of this; together, my daughter and I, learned how to pay attention to whoever was speaking into her life. We learned to be discerning, and that helped us to identify who was speaking, whether it was friend or foe!

As my daughter grew older, she learned to identify when the enemy was speaking to other people. I taught her that people were not her enemy. The Bible says, "For our struggle is not against flesh and blood, but against the rulers, against the authorities, against the powers of this dark world and against the spiritual forces of evil in the heavenly realms" (Ephesians 6:12). I told her not to struggle with people, to stay away from anyone who was cooperating with the enemy, and to pray for them. As we prayed, we saw wonderful things happen. People were changed, issues were resolved, and the enemy moved on. She learned to identify and fight the true enemy who was hiding behind the people. Further, she learned whom she could trust and whom she could not trust. This application of discernment is an important skill for life.

So remember, parents, the enemy is real. Do not just look at your kids in shock when they tell you there is a monster in their room. Do not dismiss them when they feel there is something scary under their bed. Listen and discern if they say something shocking, and obviously not from God. Children know more than we think they do when it comes to spiritual things. Do not overreact; just invite the Holy Spirit to come and help you with the situation.

Rest assured kids are quick to listen to the Spirit speak, quick to repeat what they have been told by the Spirit, and quick to act when the Spirit commands. God says, "My sheep listen to my voice; I know them, and they follow me" (John 10:29). If they are God's sheep, they know His voice, which means they can distinguish His voice from other voices they may hear. Then they will follow Him and not another. Children can call on the name of Jesus and get help really fast. They have big angels around them ready to fight!

Discernment regarding the enemy is an important skill to learn. You must teach your children how to discern their enemy when he attacks. Use the truth to fight the lies and win the battle. When you teach your children to fight lies with truth, you empower them for life. Discernment enables your children to identify the enemy, to fight him, and to obtain the victory!

8.

Knowledge – the unstoppable life giving source!

"My people are destroyed from lack of knowledge." That is what God said in Hosea 4:6. If we want to live and not be destroyed, we must learn the principles in the Bible. If we want our children to live and not be destroyed, we must teach them the principles in the Bible. Children do not know everything. They have to be taught. If we expect children to automatically honor, trust, and obey, we are expecting way too much. Children need to be taught these principles. We cannot expect to get out of them what we did not put into them. Knowledge is the eighth powerful tip for training unstoppable children.

Start teaching your children Bible principles today. Sharing, giving, and serving are a few of the many principles you can start training them from their youth. Do not assume your children know these rules. Model the Bible principles in your own life so they can observe them when they are very little. Talk about them before they are old enough to talk back. Then have them practice these principles as toddlers. When you bring knowledge into their lives, you bring truth. When you bring truth into their lives, you set them free. When children are free, they can choose to live the victorious life.

From a very young age I taught my daughter some of the principles from the Bible. One of the first principles I taught was "...the last will be first and the first will be last" (Matthew 20:16). So, anytime she was put last

I told her it was a set up for her to be put first. Every time she was not picked first for something at church or school, I told her "...the last will be first and the first will be last" (Matthew 20:16). I explained to her that being put last was a "set up" for being put first the next time. Together we prayed and reminded God what He said in his word. We looked for His promise to be fulfilled and sure enough every single time we saw God was true to His word.

This scenario happened many times throughout her childhood. Here are some examples:

- One year my daughter did not win any of the big races in a school-wide sporting event, but the day after the event her picture appeared on the front page of the local newspaper. It was one of the few pictures featured.
- On several occasions my daughter was not picked for various positions she desired in her worship group, but in the end she became a leader for the group dance rehearsals.

- One year my daughter did not think she was going to be included in the team pictures for the church magazine, but when the pictures were taken, she was front and center. That picture ended up on the cover of the magazine.
- For several years she did not get a "top" award from any of her teachers but when she got older she received the highest GPA award from her principal.

What an exciting adventure it has been—speaking God's word, believing God's Word, and watching His word fulfilled!

Another principle that I taught my daughter was the principle of giving—"Give and it will be given to you" (Luke 6:8). I taught her to give from what little money she had and wait for God to give to her. It always happened! After she gave, she would get a great coupon on the item she needed to purchase, a fantastic price on an event she wanted to attend, or an outstanding monetary reward that enabled her to obtain other things she desired. My daughter learned that the principle of sowing and reaping worked.

The general principle of sowing and reaping was expanded, to include everything in her life. In other words, I taught her that you reap whatever you sow in your life. My daughter learned that when she did something good for others, something good happened back to her. If she did something mean to others, something mean happened back to her. She realized that the principle proved true.

She often asked God for forgiveness when she did something bad to others, and together we asked God for a "crop failure" so she would not have to reap what she had sown. God, by His grace and mercy, spared my daughter many times. Because she learned the principle of sowing and reaping early in life, she had the power to create a wonderful future for her life. That is a lot of power!

As I expanded my ministry and started teaching other children the principles from the Bible, I was very nervous. I was not sure God would come through for me. I thought that if He did not come through for me, these children may start to doubt that there is a God. This whole experience was stretching my faith. I had to think about it. Was I going to take the risk and teach the entire word of God or just the parts I was sure God would answer fast? Then I realized that it was His reputation on the line, not mine. I did not need to be afraid.

I did not need to defend God; He could stand up for Himself. When I learned this one verse, "God is not a man, that he should lie, nor a son of man, that he should change his mind. Does he speak and then not act? Does he promise and not fulfill" (Numbers 23:19)? After I learned that verse, I knew I could believe everything God said in the Bible to be true. I knew I could teach everything He said! If we believe God is not a man that He should lie, we can teach anything He says as truth!

There are so many principles in the Bible that we can teach our children that it would take an entirely new book to write all of them down. These principles are available in the Bible so go look at them for yourself. Start by reading the book of Proverbs. Then go online to www.thewisdomcenter.tv and learn from one of the greatest preachers, in my opinion, on the principles of God–Dr. Mike Murdock. When you learn how to live by the principles of God, you will have a victorious life and your children will want to emulate you. Knowledge brings power–power for life!

9.

Service – the unstoppable promoter!

Jesus said, "The greatest among you will be your servant." (Matthew 23:11). He modeled service by washing his disciples' feet. Jesus set the example we want to follow. To follow Jesus is to serve people. The ninth powerful tip for training unstoppable children is service.

A part of being an active member of the "Body of Christ" is service. Once we find a church to be involved in, we can enjoy serving people in church. Yes, our kids can serve with us. When our children serve at a young age, it becomes a lifestyle for them and it sets them up for unstoppable promotion.

By the age of 2- or 3-years old children can help out with a variety of services. Little children can dance around to worship music, say amen to prayers, hold hands with someone, and the list goes on and on. Together as a family we can pass out fliers, greet people at the door, and lead kids in song and dance. There is so much we can do to serve.

In my city I found a wonderful church that has all I need for my family to serve and grow. When I walked into the church, I could tell this church was the church for my family. It just seemed like the church had "something special." That "something special" was a person, and that person's name is the Holy Spirit. I found the church I wanted to be in when I found the Holy Spirit alive and active in that church. Here is an example of His work:

One Sunday morning the Holy Spirit so moved on the pastor that he dedicated the entire service to share what the Holy Spirit had told him about the children. He shared that the Lord had told him that we have children in our church who are unstoppable for God. He called them the "Unstoppable Generation." He said these children are going to do great things for God. He shared in detail some of the great things they were going to do in the church, the city, and in the world. Then he called for all the children to be brought from the kids' church to the front of the worship center and he began to pray over them. He had his staff pray over them and anoint them. By doing this, he proved kids had value, were important, and could contribute to the "Body of Christ." He believed in the children. He believed they were going to make a difference in the church. And they do!

Imagine how I felt as a parent having witnessed my pastor speak over the children, minister to them, and expect them be able to make a difference. I was so excited I was literally jumping up and down. I knew that this pastor and this church had a destiny in mind for my daughter and for all the kids in the church. This pastor wanted them to find their purpose for being in church, their purpose for serving others, and their purpose for life! I knew right then and there it was the right church for me and my whole family.

When you find the right church, give your kids a reason to be in that church. Give your kids purpose in the church. Give your family a place in the body of Christ. When you start going to church, meet the pastor, meet the staff, and meet the main volunteers. Sign up for the "first timers" class if the church has one. Support the pastor's mission, vision, and goals. Learn more about the church so you can help them out. You can learn more by getting involved in the church.

You may want to attend weekly Bible studies, events, or socials at the church. At the same time, you will need to get your kids plugged into kids' church classes and other children's ministry programs. You never want to forget about your kids or make them feel guilty for taking time to adjust to a new routine. Also, remember never drag them to so many events that they don't have enough time to rest or play. Most of all do what you can to make church enjoyable for every member of your family. If you have a good attitude about church, they can have a good attitude about church.

Next you will need to decide in which area you want to volunteer at church. Most big churches have classes that will teach you how to discover your gifts for service. Your gifts help you to know where to volunteer. If you don't know where to start, ask God.

Do your best as a volunteer, working for the Lord. Don't just serve to get the work done. It's important! Do what you are asked to do. If they ask you to do a job that seems insignificant such as sweeping the floor, do it with pride. Remember, you are the role model for your children.

Whether you're a greeter, chauffeur, or toilet scrubber, you need to do your best work. If you do your very best, you will qualify for promotion! You'll qualify for bigger jobs – jobs that you'll really enjoy. You may qualify to be a teacher, singer, photographer, or whatever God calls you to be. He knows the desires of your heart and He will promote you when you serve with a good attitude! Your children will watch you as you serve, listen to you speak about the job, and copy what you do in church. They learn by copying you. Through your example, you can make it happen!

If at all possible, volunteer in the children's programs with your kids. Go and check out the programs and see what you can do to help. If you see problems with any of the programs, volunteer in that area and be a problem solver. People in children's ministry have a lot of work to do, and they need problem solvers to help them. They do not need people who cause problems. Remember you are the church. The kids programs are only as good as the volunteers who run them.

When you and your kids serve the church, you will benefit in many ways. When my family and I started serving in church programs, we immediately began reaping the benefits of serving. We got so many benefits from volunteering, it was surprising.

First of all, we got to do what we loved doing and we did not really have to be experts at it either. I enjoyed dancing around to music; it was fun! When the ministry leaders found out that I liked dancing, they asked me to lead worship. I did not say I was good at it, I just liked it. When they asked me to lead worship, I thought other people would be lining up to do that job but I was wrong. Nobody was doing that job! In Children's Ministry they usually need so much help that if you are willing and have a good attitude, you can pretty much volunteer where you want, doing what you enjoy.

The next benefit our family received was that my child got to serve alongside of me in ministry. While she was still young, my daughter started helping me and together we lead worship in the kids' church program. At that point, she became so involved in our church that she never wanted to miss a Sunday. We never had to fight about going to church—a dream come true!

Another benefit is that my whole family had wonderful Christian mentors working alongside of us to guide and direct, honor and respect us. It was powerful having ministry leaders mentoring our family. One other perk I received was a free education in ministry. I learned so much about ministry just by serving. As I was faithful in service, I was given higher levels of responsibilities in the church. In other words, I was promoted.

I was offered a job at the church in Children's Ministry which was a blessing to my entire family. I had been promoted and was now being paid for what I loved to do. I didn't even have to ask for a job; the job came to me.

I did not even have to interview for this job. I just filled out the paper work. I was not looking for a job but service brings promotion. Promotion brings rewards!

I learned many other things in service. From the kids' church curriculum, I learned many Bible stories that I used to teach my child at home. From the worship music and materials, I learned to conduct worship at home. Since I had to study and prepare for church, I brought many materials home; my daughter received the benefit of all the wonderful "kid-friendly" worship music, ministry tools, and teaching materials right in the comfort of her own home. With these materials, I practiced by conducting kids' church in my living room every week.

My daughter's involvement in church increased as we began attending practice on Wednesdays, Saturdays, and early some Sunday mornings. Pretty much anytime there were kids' programs running in our church, we were involved.

Then my husband got involved in managing the technical and sound booths for the children's ministry and became best friends with the children's pastor. From that point, he was receiving training, mentorship, and friendship from a staff pastor. How cool is that!

Because my daughter was also serving, she experienced promotion herself. My daughter began leading in worship, Bible club, and events. She acted on stage, performed with puppets, led groups in prayer, choreographed dances, and taught worship to peers all before she reached the age of 12.

She assisted teachers, leaders, and directors at church. After that she received more promotion and position in her school. She made the Honor roll numerous times, received the highest GPA twice, and was voted Chaplain of Student Council twice. She was lined up for promotion, and she got it. She is still a leader among her peers. God has done amazing things in her life and I am overjoyed.

You too can experience the joy of having children who are lined up for promotion. If you embrace the act of service, your children can follow your lead and also be promoted well beyond normal levels of leadership at a very young age. Service does indeed lead to promotion and this type of promotion is unstoppable!

10.

Belief – the unstoppable dream maker!

Believe what God believes about your children. God believes in children. God has special plans for them, plans for now and in the future. In His grace He has called them out to be his own. Here is one example of a child being called out by God: God said to Jeremiah, the son of Hilkiah the priest, "Before I formed you in the womb I knew you, before you were born I set you apart; I appointed you as a prophet to the nations" (Jeremiah 1:5). God predicted the future of many of His children.

Do you have dreams for your children? Do you have dreams of them fulfilling their purpose in life? Do you want them to be all that God has called them to be? If you would like to know what God has called them to be, you need to ask Him what He wants them to do. You need to ask God to prophesy over each one of your children. Believe what He tells you about your children. If you know what God believes they are called to be, you can prepare them to do what they are destined to do. Belief is the tenth powerful tip for training unstoppable children.

Because I wanted to know how to train my child, I asked God to tell me what He believed about her. In other words, I asked Him to prophesy over her. God is so good He answered my prayer. He revealed to me what He believed about my daughter.

God sent a lady to my house to prophesy over my daughter. That lady did not even know she was prophesying or she might have been a little nervous! She saw my daughter holding a toy microphone singing to people in my house, and she proclaimed "So your daughter is going to be a worship leader." In that instant, I remembered that I had asked God to prophesy. As soon as I heard the words she said, I believed it. God had sent that lady to tell me my daughter was going to be a worship leader!

Because I believed what God said, the prophecy totally came true. My child joined a worship team for children. She led worship and eventually became a very strong leader among leaders. Because I believed what God said about my child, it came to pass. And now, I can't stop believing great things for my daughter every day!

Do not believe what the Devil tells you about your children. Do not trust the Devil. The Devil is a liar! He may be trying to tell you that your children are going to be like the prodigal son who spent so much time running away from God and ended up in a pigpen before coming to his senses. The Devil may have tried to tell you that your children are too weak, too young, or too silly to be what God wants them to be. Do not listen to him!

Do not think about what your children can not do right now. Focus on what God says they can do in the future. If God, who is the perfect Father, does not stare at your inadequacies, don't stare at your children's inadequacies. If God believes in your success, you need to believe in your children's success. Think about it this way: you are God's child; He believes in you and trusts you to raise your children. So then, think about what God does and consider trusting your children with the work God has given them to do.

Speak the true word of God over your children, not the words of doubt and fear. The word of God is powerful and He says, "…my word that goes out from my mouth: It will not return to me empty, but will accomplish what I desire and achieve the purpose for which I sent it" (Isaiah 55:11). That means if God gives you a word for your children, it will come true!

Moses believed what God said about the children of Israel. Moses believed they would be free because God said they would be free. Because Moses believed it, he was able to lead the people out of slavery. At first, Aaron did not believe in the children of Israel. In the book of Exodus, God shows us what Aaron thought about his people. He doubted them. He doubted they would follow the one true God. Aaron's doubt became a reality when Moses went up the mountain and meet with God.

The people asked Aaron for an idol to follow because Moses was not there to lead them. They were looking for a leader, someone to lead them into the Promised Land. Aaron could have filled in as a temporary leader for the people while Moses was gone. Aaron could have led the people to worship the one true God, but he did not. Instead, he made a false god for them to follow. Aaron made a golden calf for them, and then he built an altar around that calf so the people could bow down and worship it!

When Moses returned from the mountain he saw the golden calf. Moses was shocked at what had happened; he asked Aaron, "What did these people do to you, that you led them into such great sin" (Exodus 32:21)? You would have thought that they had hog tied Aaron and pinned him to the ground until he did what they asked him to do, but that was not the case. Aaron told Moses, "You know how prone these people are to evil. They said to me 'Make us gods who will go before us. As for this fellow Moses who brought us up out of Egypt, we don't know what has happened to him'" (Exodus 32: 22-23).

The problem was Aaron believed that the people were "prone to evil." God did not say the people were prone to evil; Aaron did. God said they were "stiff-necked" people (Exodus 32:9) and there is big difference between a "stiff-necked" people and a people "prone to evil." Based on Aaron's doubt of the children of Israel, he led all of them into the sin of idol worship! Let us not make the same mistake— believing our children are "prone to evil."

Now, ask yourself what you believe about your children. Do you believe they are evil, stupid, or lazy? These are strong words. You may not actually be saying these words about your kids, but do you believe these words? Examine your belief system. Are you a doubter? If you doubt your children all the time, your thoughts of doubt are going to show up in your behavior. You will think like a doubter, sound like a doubter, and act like a doubter.

The Bible says, "...know the truth, and the truth will set you free" (John 8:32). The sooner you confront any of the negative beliefs you may have about your children, the sooner you can dismantle these negative thoughts, and replace them with positive thoughts. Start thinking about the great plans God has for your children. God wants you to trust that He has good plans for them. The Bible says, "'For I know the plans I have for you,' declares the Lord, 'plans to prosper you and not to harm you, plans to give you hope and a future'" (Jeremiah 29:11). You can trust God. He has great plans for your children!

Now that you've exposed the doubts in your mind, you need to change your focus. Start to focus on your children's successes, even the little ones. Any little accomplishment in your children's lives should be celebrated in some way. Take the time to recognize all the little things your children have done. Talking about the things your children have accomplished is a way of celebrating them. Celebrate with a smile, a hug, your time, a small gift, or an act of service. You don't have to throw a major party every time they cross a "t" or dot an "i," but you do need to place value on the little achievements. It will change your focus.

When you change your focus from failure to success, you will change the lives of your children. Your children will change their focus from negative to positive.

Whatever you do, make sure you are not continually reviewing their mistakes. Think of it this way, if God's focus was on your mistakes, you would feel so condemned. It would stop you dead in your tracks, and you would not be able to do anything right. Besides, it is not fun to be around anybody who focuses on your fears and failures. If you doubt your children all the time, they will not want to be around you!

Before I learned that believing in my child was so important, I did not believe in her. I loved her. I would do anything for her. But I did not believe in her. When I doubted my daughter, I acted like a doubter. I worried all the time, I grilled her with questions, and I micromanaged her life. The Bible says that "...the letter (of the law) kills, but the Spirit of God gives life" (2 Corinthians 3:6). My focus was death not life.

In fact, I walked in such great fear that my child would fail, that she did fail. I was afraid she would do wrong all the time. I sat at home just imagining my child doing wrong things. I wondered if she had any interest in God at all. I was a strong doubter! I doubted my daughter so much that fear and failure were at the center of my thoughts and focus for her life. How sad was that?

When God corrected me, He showed me that I was so concentrated on my daughter's failure that I had lifted her failure up to the highest place in my mind. Fear was exalted so high that it was like a god to me. The Bible says, "We demolish arguments and every pretension that sets itself up against the knowledge of God, and we take captive every thought to make it obedient to Christ" (2 Corinthians 10:5). That means we don't let our minds worry; we make our minds trust.

The minute I made the choice to change my mind, everything changed. I began to trust God. When I put all my focus on Him and began to worship Him, He came into the picture and brought with Him everything I needed for my child. When God came in, my daughter had the grace and power she needed to succeed. When I changed my thinking, I changed my daughter. I worshiped God instead of worshiping fear. I believed what God believed and ignored fear. I believed in her. I was set free and my daughter was set free. You too can be set free! You can trust God. You can expect the best! When you teach your children that you believe in them, they can believe in themselves.

You can stop doubting and start believing in them today and it will change the course of their lives forever! Believe in your children. Then they can believe in themselves. You can do it! Do it right now! Believe in them now! Their future is at stake!

God believed in people so much that He created them in His image. When you look at your children, you can see the face of God looking back at you. If God believes in them, we can believe in them. Believing in our children makes their dreams come true!

Remember, it is important to equip your children to be unstoppable. If you train them to be unstoppable, they will push through the attacks of the enemy to obtain the victory every time. The most important mission field you will enter is your home. Now, go to the field and accomplish the first mission God has given you: "Train up a child in the way he should go, and when he is old he will not turn from it" (Proverbs 22:6).

Thank you so much for reading this book. May God richly bless you for caring for His children!

Patti Gibble has a Master of Education degree and Bachelor of Arts in Education. She is a trained ministry worker who has directed Children's worship and Kids' church programs at a mega church. Patti grew up in Orlando, Florida where she worked at Disney World. She now writes books and spends time with the Holy Spirit in Tucson, Arizona.

12462521R00053

Made in the USA
Charleston, SC
06 May 2012